MAGNIFICENT ERRORS

THE ERNEST SANDEEN PRIZE IN POETRY

Editors
Joyelle McSweeney, Orlando Menes

2022	*Magnificent Errors*, Sheryl Luna
2019	*Splinters Are Children of Wood*, Leia Penina Wilson
2017	*Among Ruins*, Robert Gibb
2015	*Underdays*, Martin Ott
2013	*The Yearning Feed*, Manuel Paul López
2011	*Dream Life of a Philanthropist*, Janet Kaplan
2009	*Juan Luna's Revolver*, Louisa A. Igloria

Editor, John Matthias (1997–2007)

2007	*The Curator of Silence*, Jude Nutter
2005	*Lives of the Sleepers*, Ned Balbo
2003	*Breeze*, John Latta
2001	*No Messages*, Robert Hahn
1999	*The Green Tuxedo*, Janet Holmes
1997	*True North*, Stephanie Strickland

MAGNIFICENT ERRORS

SHERYL LUNA

University of Notre Dame Press
Notre Dame, Indiana

University of Notre Dame Press
Notre Dame, Indiana 46556
undpress.nd.edu

Copyright © 2022 by Sheryl Luna

All Rights Reserved

Published in the United States of America

Library of Congress Control Number: 2021948614

ISBN: 978-0-268-20181-4 (Hardback)
ISBN: 978-0-268-20182-1 (Paperback)
ISBN: 978-0-268-20180-7 (WebPDF)
ISBN: 978-0-268-20183-8 (Epub)

For Dawn and Zenon

CONTENTS

Acknowledgments   ix

I

Lowering Your Standards for Food Stamps   3
The Vocation   4
The Thief   5
Change   6
Tornillo's Tent Prison for Migrant Children   8
Salt Shaker   9
Meditation on Hunger   10
Breathing the Border's Fire   11
The Poet   13
Autumn's Art   14
Forehead   16
regeneration   18
What I'd Say If I Had Fifteen Minutes of Fame   19

II

Shock and Awe   23
Neighbors Smoke on an Apartment Porch
Owned by a Mental Health Agency   24
Secret Missionary for the Virgin Mary Off His Meds   26
The Sailing Bicycle   28
Shock Treatment   29
Lit   31

Lamentation to Praise   34
The Language of Drowning   35
The Star Song   36
To Rest   37
The Leaves   38
Manic with Depression   39
Eccentric   41
A Homeless Poet Friend Rages at the World's Lesser People   42
The Party   43
Adopting Stepfather   45
Alone   46
Voice   48
Figures   50
Anxiety and Diagnosis   51
The Artist Addressing Violence   52
The Singer   53
She Wishes She Never Had   54
IQ Over 160?   55
The Prayer   56

III

Night   59
Rubbernecking   60
Listening to Sky   61
Risk   63
The Laugh   65
We Believe in Kindness Because It's Hard to Die   66
Casualties   67
The Witness   68
The Hummingbird   69
Clouds and Sapling   70
Prayer for This Clay Earth   71
Mud   72
Finding Water   74
The Transgression   75

ACKNOWLEDGMENTS

I would like to thank the judges of the Ernest Sandeen Poetry Prize, Orlando Menes and Joyelle McSweeney, for choosing the collection, the University of Notre Dame English Department, and the University of Notre Dame Press. I would also like to thank the many poets and writers and friends and family who made this collection possible, and whose encouragement I am forever grateful for: Dagoberto Gilb, Joy Roulier Sawyer, and Ray Gonzalez for the kind blurbs, Carmen Seda, Christine Granados, Fran Ford, Amit Ghosh, Dawn Grochocki, Zenon Grochocki, Rachel and Alberto Escamilla, Shirley and Richard Garcia, Paul Gutierrez, Lew Forester, Martin Balgach, Madelyn Garner, Andrea Watson, Leslie Ullman, Marie C. Jones, Michael Henry, the Lighthouse Writer's Workshop, The Denver Foundation, Texas Institute of Letters, Hard Times Writing Workshop, the gamuts, and of course, always and forever, my steadfast support, my mother Ida.

The following poems have been published or are forthcoming in the following magazines, sometimes in a previous form.

"Shock and Awe," "The Thief," "Lowering Your Standards for Food Stamps," "The Vocation," and "Neighbors Smoke on an Apartment Porch Owned by a Mental Health Agency" *Poetry*

"Rubbernecking" *Plough Quarterly*

"The Leaves" *Cardinal Sins Journal*

"Mud" originally published "The Text" *Taos Journal of International Poetry and Art*

"Alone" *Magnolia*

"Night" *Puerto del Sol*

"Change" and "The Star Song" *Pilgrimage Magazine*

"Lit" and "The Singer" (as "The Singer Finds Variations of Her Voice") *Saranac Review*

"Secret Missionary for the Virgin Mary Off His Meds," "The Sailing Bicycle," "The Party," and "Shock Treatment" *Huizache*

"The Witness" and "The Transgression" *America Magazine*

"She Wishes She Never Had" *Birdy*

"To Rest," "Anxiety and Diagnosis," and "Prayer for this Clay Earth" *Denver Voice*

"Forehead" *Chiricó*

"The Poet" *ZYZZYVA*

"Tornillo's Tent Prison for Migrant Children" and "Casualties" *Poetry Is Currency*

I

The purpose of art is washing the dust of daily life off our souls.
—Pablo Picasso

Lowering Your Standards for Food Stamps

Words fall out of my coat pocket,
soak in bleach water. I touch everyone's
dirty dollars. Maslow's got everything on me.
Fourteen hours on my feet. No breaks.
No smokes or lunch. Blank-eyed movements:
trash bags, coffee burner, fingers numb.
I am hourly protestations and false smiles.
The clock clicks its slow slowing.
Faces blur in a stream of hurried soccer games,
sunlight and church certainty. I have no
poem to carry, no material illusions.
Cola spilled on hands, so sticky fingered,
I'm far from poems. I'd write of politicians,
refineries and a border's barbed wire,
but I am unlearning America's languages
with a mop. In a summer-hot red
polyester top, I sell lotto tickets. Cars wait for gas
billowing black. Killing time has new meaning.
A jackhammer breaks apart a life. The slow globe
spirals, and at night black space has me dizzy.
Visionaries off their meds and wacked out
meth heads sing to me. A panicky fear of robbery
and humiliation drips with my sweat.
Words some say are weeping twilight and sunrise.
I am drawn to dramas, the couple arguing, the man
head-butting his wife in the parking lot.
911: no metered aubade, and nobody but
myself to blame.

The Vocation

Lit with strange carpentry magic—
they build timeshares in her head, carve
names deep in wood, erect beams of metal to hold up
the invincible defense of a bad history. They mourn
what's subjective. They are shutters, closed.
Sometimes I imagine such men in flip flops
with fat towels draped over confident shoulders.
I imagine they all live in Texas, and find
South Padre too hot, and then I imagine them blaming
diversity for everything. Here, in the middle of grief,
we pout to the rhythm of their sentences.
Suns hiss in their dreams. Soon such critics will meet
daily for prayers. The Pharisees identify the guilty woman.
They are gathering sticks for a witch burning. Curandera
lit with the fire of sighs, casts spells, burns sage,
sweats in a lodge, her own prayers flaming.

The Thief

I am not saying "mark my words,"
as the thief says early each winter.
He leaves nothing of value. He too wants.
A brute with language, he has a fondness
for preaching. I am bathed to luster.
Memories move musically through my bones.
He sings above, vaults off a horse with feigned
kindness, lands so fancy. Letting go of this,
sitting with tropical leaves the size of men
in a terrarium, I am beautiful. He means well
admonishing women. He is lucky
with the show of crankiness.
What does it mean to let go the envy?
I sometimes hope stars don't spread themselves
over New York's lights. Performing for himself,
glasses glittering, he reads stories of poverty,
claims them all as his own.
Here in Colorado, irises of all colors unfold
outwards to the half-hidden sun. On the cracked
cement, chilly before rain, I see perpetual
beginnings. I'm going to forget him:
lock him in a box in my head,
lock him in the haunt of violins, let go what's his
in the hurl of breath in my groans.

Change

I've cast away a thousand stones.
Turning with the moon, I am no longer sketching
sombreros and Day of the Dead candy skulls.

I've long divorced the speech of wild assurance.
Winter will be blowing soon enough.

Resting in the sweep of church bells, my throat
no longer tight, I repeat myself, vote myself, sing myself.

I have let go the gang-banger talk, the appearances of protest.
I've secretly begun to unwind to Mozart. I write to Für Elise.

Translated no longer by wealthy men, I am unforgiving.
I am no longer enamored with the sunshine bleeding over Juárez hills.

I no longer apologize for the sky changing its hue, for my voice
flailing and scraping through cultures. I am not conceptual.

Woodwinds sing. I have torn open my shame.
People in this town love a falling.
We have seen each other as ghosts. I refuse to fly flags.

We have ways with one another: clipped language,
staccato need and expectation. Self-proclaimed radicals
seize nothing in me. The unfair world glistens and numbs.

Beyond theories and histories, I am darkening.
I am no longer contracted by bigots or false martyrs.
There is no purity within; I am mixed —a bloody Mary.

I am dirty and willfully calm to Pachelbel's Canon in D.
There is no shadow of repression today, comrades and brothers.

Sisters, I have lost my lunge and refuse to linger in cliques.
I am unkempt. My hair in the breeze makes its own music.

Tornillo's Tent Prison for Migrant Children

There's a compulsion to sing of ranches outside El Paso
where cumbias and gritos keep everyone happy.
Meditating on the familiar, I remember the fence,
the border and being alone. Better to be in the open
desert than caged. Men in rags once slept on our lawn.
Look, I am honoring men and mothers who cry.
Tornillo, a tent city, 471 parents deported
without their children. Pesos traded for freedom
that never came. What is it that divides us?
A fence, metal reaching high to the sky
along a highway or hate? Juárez's huge Mexican flag
flaps nearby. I walk down a sandy
path. All that is familiar, a mirage.
There is only one pond in El Paso at Ascarate park.
The ducks there thin and hungry for more than bread.
The powerful have the strongest appetite.
The buildings are teaching us all things fall.
The demagogue bites cleanly.
If I could calm the angry mob,
and send Mexico a song, I would.
The Rio Grande a slow drying hope. The Santa Fe Bridge
and its crossers know what we don't or won't.
The deportees are seeking tenderness,
the shadow on the wall of the oval office berates
the universe. How bitterly we argue or remain silent.

Salt Shaker

I too have been shaken,
spilled, crystalized, scattered.
I have lived in a glass jar
with a tin lid,

the sounds of dinner talk
muffled and echoing
through my broken body.

If you touch what is left
of me, I am but a grainy
texture, something to be
sprinkled on something else—

I am meant to add flavor, sass,
to spice the world up, to give up
my body for another and lend what's
broken a healing balm.

Snow-like I fall over the world
molecular, dazzling like
forgiveness, like compassion.

The whole of *me* long lost
in the space of what was
dead sea, Indian ocean,
the march of one man refusing

violence against the earth.
Half-naked in sandals, Gandhi,
walked the salt march, each footprint
a light step kissing the ground.

Meditation on Hunger

One poet sings within, another poet cries.
Childlike they paint
with the sway of warm colors.

Hungry for being heard, their words
rivulet unnoticed. They speak more smog
than substance. Nobody's listening,
everyone clamoring for their own.

Desiring awards, laughter and applause,
their poems lay unread, so they hunger

further into the music of loss,
until they begin to ripen
on the ground, so sweet below
everything they desire.

Breathing the Border's Fire

The border, a fence, a desert, bodies

    scattered like cacti. The river too swollen blue with them

    And yet   *How beautiful the sadness of crows*

Whistling children wake me from dreams

I have rushed through decades

    split like an orange torn apart for strangers

    Days I felt sliced like a bleeding catfish gutted

    There were my rants, the rants of others

I rose a tide against Chicano allies   so afraid I was of trust

My eyes brown with the histories of maternal Natives blinked

I missed ribbons of light   marooned near catfish skeletons and trash

        But I began to plant   I plowed for years

Squash sprouted, enough to feed centuries of women

        I choose at times to bop to cumbias, rancheras

breath-filled and sweaty

Large wind chimes still sing in my mind

It's as if there is an eternal

heat rolling over me,

forearms drenched in sweat

days swaying

    like the last trees

waving goodbye to a fiery wind

The Poet

after Martin Balgach

He is an astronomer
measuring the distance
between light and loneliness,
time and silence, the sound of his voice
and the dreams of millions.
There are constellations in his eyes,
and orphaned poems fill his days.
He holds his face in his palms every night.
Universes wander inside him. He feels
himself a black hole, space, the extraterrestrial
other. The real mystery is love and he
deems the indifferent galaxies expanding
forever into nothingness, a kind of perfect
stillness. He calculates wishes
and lost dreams, draws conclusions
and arguments based on hunger and the empty
stomach of humanity. The moon is an idea
and light shimmers on the rough water
of himself, running into a sea gray
with the polluted madness of want.
He believes in firecrackers, the supernova
of desire's fight against time, but he knows
it's all a lie. There is the rumor
of salvation. He wants to hold
onto the last warmth of the sun,
to believe his small yelp matters,
that the Milky Way mourns his passing,
burns stardust while his hands are lit
with a million years of truth.

Autumn's Art

Envious poets

die like sunflowers in October,

heavy-headed, they fall towards ground.

At some point, stampede and propaganda call.

The oeuvre warns me, I'm not alone.

The sliced moon glints the edge of my iris.

Don't ask a question you know the answer to.

Whirlwind of secret need: my desire to be heard.

I'm half lie, half mask, wild orchestra.

My branches grow jagged, split, touch the sky's

emptiness. To be an artist is to be

afraid, to be one is to be at once open and closed.

To be an artist is to find one's breath, to see ego

vanish into the dusk. I'm not there yet, seeking oblivion

in each word. I seek deliverance from my plumed stance.

There are meditations on death.

Each begins in love. There's something to an evocation,

a forgetting of this hungry Self.

Forehead

after Andrés Montoya

I too am a Romantic
despite it being uncool.
I too have a scar,
but mine cascades across
my brow unevenly. The mystery
of the single line shocked me
when I fell hard onto tile as a child—
hematoma, tumor. Your forehead
a great wall of song. My scar
a third eye, yours a valley
where eyebrows wept at its feet.
There were days the sorrow
of my own scar sunk into a frown.
I imagined the loss of my birth father
there in the falling, in the breaking.
It was in the rolling music of loss
where I found the scar fading into
a lighter tone than the wall of my skin.
It was as if it had freed itself in a quiet rest,
a softening sound, healing from the rumbling
waves of myself. You, Andrés, said you hoped
your scar would produce a symphony of sighs.
I would settle for the silences between
what is beautiful, or the shy smiles between
the moan of violas. The point was, I think,
what is broken, heals. What is blooded, seals.
Even the sky, when seemingly cracked and lit aflame
cools itself with rain, and I go on too long, Andrés.
I forget you and your late leukemia poems—

where you were left to "study the poisoned blood
of [your] own heart," seeking all the while
the song of a single bird. You sang of a God
who fell in love with your eyes, your hair,
the blush of your cheeks, and I imagine,
even your scar.

regeneration

after Andrés Montoya

I too lit one after another, a chain of hurt towards my own death.
Andrés when you wrote about him sucking a pipe's
blackness into his lungs, I imagined him being
your friend. You said he saw his brother beaten
to death, and the closest thing I could imagine to it
was my cousin Joey sucker-punching David Barone
in the guts, hard, but David didn't cry, he was too startled.
He held his belly as he slid down to his knees, and Joe
left impassive, telling Barone to pick on people his own size
since David had pounded Joe's little brother down.
Joe always had a cigarette dangling from his pursed teenage lips.
He was embroiled with the entire world. There was no kindness.
And Andrés, it was your friend sucking on a pipe, red flame
a small moon. You wrote of his ragged clothes, nearby gunfire
and your sister rocking a small child. You had it right, while
inhaling smoke, "everything begins to fade in a haze of adrenalin."
For years I smoked to forget my father's hands.
For years Joe smoked to forget his father's fists.
For years the man in your poem smoked to forget the pool of blood his
    brother died in.
Smoke is the gray exhale of loss.
It's the way one numbs to forget poverty.
Now, when I breathe clear-lunged and unbroken, I feel blessed
to walk city streets. You wrote that they called him a spic Andrés,
but he was holy the way a priest blesses a congregation of fools
with incense. When someone dies, we continue to speak to them.
We were all cut with moments of grace and know he reveled
in the sweet aroma of smoky rings and gray feathered clouds.

What I'd Say If I Had Fifteen Minutes of Fame

Gandhi's grandson throwing a too short
pencil away, desiring a new freshly sharpened one.
Gandhi making him find the old one in the dark,
in the trash out back, telling him waste is
violence done to the world. It's quite unpoetic—
Modify your thoughts, sit in the four corners
of the earth, watch open sky breathe its last.
High in the hills, streams lit with sun tell a story,
water rushing, sounding its ancient call.
Your face warm in the light, bare feet cool.
There's nothing perilous here in the West
while we bomb the hell out of *them*. Yet,
each footprint a light step kissing ground.

II

*One must still have chaos in oneself to be able
to give birth to a dancing star.*

—Friedrich Nietzsche

Shock and Awe

Tightened jaw, I did not love.
Flashback of myself jerked about,
legs high above my head, men
laughing, I came to sea drifts,
movement and crashing. I found I am
not so far from God exploding.
Gifting, a friend once said, is why we live.
Seven storks white and still on a gold lake.
My lazy eye glances back to that original
split, myself high above myself.
Whiplashed into forgetting, I didn't know
hours from minutes. I was hyper-vigilant
for catastrophes: my head raging then numb.
The early garden bare, and now,
shocked with sudden memory,
I return to changing sky hues,
blooms of lilac bursting along sidewalks.
Lazy in the grass, I free myself of guilt,
imagine musicians in the park, us overcoming
ourselves. My eyes open before stars.
Holy these leaves, these skies.
What is torn
opens for light.

Neighbors Smoke on an Apartment Porch Owned by a Mental Health Agency

Dazed with rambling gossip,
they are at odds with indifference.

There is their looming net of mistakes,
their love of rumor.

A gull darts over and behind
bare buildings. They all dream arousal,

shaggy forests, mountains, city streets.
Trees lose leaves, and one manic man

insists the leaves aren't dying after
collecting outdated food at church.

Upswing in full euphoric force, he's
certain he's spreading world peace.

Oaks yellow. Rocks trap leaves.
Men at work lumber to dumpsters.

Their language bellows need.

Jehovah Witnesses mouthed salvation
Monday to Janice. She listened wishful,

but today relays her own bitter story:
lazy sister-in-law fat on a couch,

quarter-sized bedsores on her ass,
brother-in-law blind, stumbling drunk.

Hearts rigid and numb, they forget
crepe myrtle blooming pink.

Impermanent and frenetic worry hums.
Eyes grow glaucoma blue. Sucking

cigarettes and mumbling, they stand
hardy as an autumn day's
geraniums, hard before winter.

Secret Missionary for the Virgin Mary Off His Meds

He writes of grenades, a universe exploding.

It's inexhaustible, the sky. Something about badness
turns him on. Passion, a candle with two wicks.

He says to me, "keep burning."
He often falls out of love,

handles language like a theologian, misses
lilies. Lately he insists fall's leaves aren't dead.

His knowledge flickers brown-bagged, like rows
of luminaria candles at night. Seasonal
Affective, he deals with feminine questions.

He argues without hearing his own voice.

Within an occasional dream, he hears language
glide along the starched collars of men.

He will not let himself show sadness or joy.
He forgets the late afternoon lake
golden, geese calling out in droves.

No gang-banger, his past is a series of commitments,
seventy-four-hour holds, Haldol and Seroquel.
Now refusing meds,

he's found the weather quite bothersome.
Wringing his hands to a fallen image of God,
he has a hurried urgency to be uninvolved.

Like a man in solitary confinement
in prison tossing shit to the guards,

he refuses to smile. Know-it-all criticisms of others
make his days. He cannot let go atheism or disbelief.

Electroshock therapy has him grasping at a forgotten past.
He walks lanky towards a loneliness he won't refuse.

And the aftermath of madness is calm.

He tries to forget the dread of monotony and expectation.

We, with the same steps, trod towards some understanding,
some philosophy. All of us, keepers of secrets.

The Sailing Bicycle

A Russian man sandpapers the bark of a dead tree
seeking to reawaken beauty. Later, homeless in
rollerblades with walking sticks made of golf clubs,

tennis balls for each base, his head half-shaven,
he asks, "Where has my wife fled?" Blaming her greed,
he is a swarm of reflections. Sky huddles about him.

Rims of clouds pink at twilight, trees the darkening
frame. He's removed tile from his bathroom for odd
reasons, and the landlord has kicked him out. He lit
trees on fire barbequing, flames eight feet tall. He erects

a hang gliding sail on his bicycle with a plumbing pipe.
Blue, it catches the wind. They call him schizophrenic;
he'll have none of that. In bright yellow-leafed madness,
squirrels dart fitfully to half-eaten pumpkins.
Clouds today a gray crowd.

Someone is weeping, but not Vladimir; he finds an airport
runway. Cops tell him to please take apart his apparatus.
Complying, he tells them America is about money's power.

Shock Treatment

for Ross

Yesterday the quiet monks in his head sang out.

An angry man with schizophrenia said, "It's hard to lose weight on meds,"
told the world to fuck off. He had a name, called me lady,
asked me later what I was writing, if I was with the feds.

He repeated himself over and over, said, "It's hard to lose weight."
Yesterday was the first day of his resurrection to peace, the last
day of his reckoning with time. The man did not rise phoenix-like.

Cigarette smoke streamed through him as if he were exhaust in the blue.
Before he died, he grabbed a golf club in a room, said he was struck
by lightning using it the day before. He stole language from ghosts,

came off shock treatments losing memories. His honesty arrived
dark and blunt. It arrived as the clearing of a throat, smoker's cough.

Before the shocks, he was lonesome for friends, eyes blue.
After the shocks, he was lonesome for friends, eyes gray.

After he couldn't remember what people said, dizzy with uncoordination,
eyes always on the blank past. He imagined he did something wrong.

Karma, he said, was out to get him. He prayed for himself the way a coach
screams at an athlete. What does it mean if he fell, struck his heavy head,
died? I am praying for his dead soul, trying to believe in the madness

of traffic, in the struggling suspicions that always tilted his gray head.
Is he a joyous quiet now, forever grateful, no longer pissed a stranger
moved the coffee pot, hid his phone charger, messed with his radio?

Paranoia plodded his last days, stalked him like a weatherman
casting spells over worries, stormed his misery. He died cremated,
buried in a mausoleum he feared. His own parents buried there

half a century. Its tall whiteness stretches into Colorado
sky, blocking a western view of the Rockies. How he hated it there,
monolithic, dead, bodies, skeletons, ashes, stacked one by one in a great
theatre of insignificance, a silence he couldn't bear.

Lit

Once my left eye mysteriously sealed shut,
doctors were at a loss to my blindness. Thin robins

ran across a dusky lawn when my stepfather died. Split
back to childhood rape, his old voice told me
no one would believe me. Much later,

I was Buddha-less, Christ didn't help me see.
Fogged and misreading the universe, I held

nothing in my palm. Jaw-clenched,
moving with fear, I ran the world in red shoes.

*

Tumbleweed and huizache tough, I rolled
up streets. Thirst came.

Faces swarmed as bees; there were no trees.
Chain-smoking, I drew myself too large.

*

After jagged flashbacks and sunlight,
I saw the haze after a hundred-degree day cool,
smelled desert after rainstorm, saw wildflowers
bloom.

*

Now, learning the ways of rivers and sunlight, I dance
Wounded-Knee remembrance. Baptized in desert after rain,

thirst quelled, I hear more than drums. Globe
willows can be found in my eyes. My tongue quiet.

*

Crickets and voices sound off.
I cut seven-foot sunflowers down this autumn,

their faces drooping for winter. I cut a yellow
garden down, cut down the past.

Planting chrysanthemums and small pines,

memory and truth collided. My jack-hammered soul
rests after remembering my father's hands.

Healing zigzags, loops, returns

flies outward to the night, then sun.

Recovery strays, finds it way home.

*

Eye soothed now, I see more than moon and sunset.

Losing this self is madness. I see lit windows,
people dancing as shadows. Purple rooms in my house

shout glory. I feel I can almost touch the lips of strangers.
My face is clean. My eyes clear and tearless.

I have visions of thriving women. Oaks toss their leaves
miraculously gold and red. The desert rests
ready for winter. I too drink new waters,

walk through houses with no doors, only open spaces
to enter. Ravens caw in flight. My losses always rebound;
there's only now, this winter of light.

Lamentation to Praise

        Startled by trauma,

I touch no one,

hear only the silence of forgetting,

        talk endlessly but speak to no one.

When I remember childhood rape, it is with clarity.

        Decades after disremembering, it all comes back.

        Do you want the details? I won't tell you.

Tonight, a fox runs the streets shaggy, thin, and skittish.

        A burgeoning moon fractures the lake.

I paint trees with pink, blue and purple leaves;

        seasons drift like a refrain of thoughts.

When I remember shock, it is as sunset, an early moon

        hanging on to the light.

The Language of Drowning

When a child is gang-raped,
stepfather led,
she can see forever when the world spins.

In every old photograph, she smiles
gap-toothed beyond the lens into
forgetting.

What cracks open
beauty like pain?

Crazed birds call. She hums with traffic.

Believing is singing in first person.

She's a sky, river-currents, sun.

Finding the words, new
sentences dream her back
from invisibility.

She knows a hawk grasps a small
dying animal, talons break a thin neck.

She knows some survive, thrive,
grow to hunt. The heart

turns in its abrupt seasons. Lit yellow
daisies cling firmly to earth

in early fall's wind. And every
half-barren bush holds on
to its fiery life for a time.

The Star Song

Windshield blind with blades and thick rain, I hear

    a woman singing alone.

        Crows fall out of the sky.

    People see and gather to watch. Memory

ricochets through all of us.

        Tobacco black, I was once dangerous. Loud.

Manifesting for a time. A match lit briefly. I am wide awake.

      Letting go tonight   rain clears,

and the desert smells like a crisp

      peony. Stars grow

New Mexico large.   I rouse

    night's black monsoon,

            lighting my own star.

To Rest

The A&D Motel on West Colfax,
Mental Health Center hotel voucher,
torn up carpet, small fridge.
I'm thankful, despite the old woman
running the place, telling
the maintenance man
I broke the toilet—
"She's mental," she says,
finger pointed towards her small head.
Yet I am joyous; I laugh.
First time I've caught luck,
compassion. The warm spring's
wildflowers peak from rocks along
cracked white stucco walls of the place.
I am free, a new belief in karma.
Transitional housing comes my way.
My life broad turn. I am opening to sky
and light. A steady check coming soon.
Rhythm without strain, a windblown face
eager to risk shame. The world needs
stories, the world needs breath and starlight.
We are all headed home, after all.

The Leaves

Meticulously penciling leaves, she is slow
time in a windowless room. She says she's known
rivers forever. There's a red sun in her mouth.
Mourning for trees, she sketches each leaf's dark,
erases veins a dozen times. We fall into spaces,
into forms. What's unseen is as important as what's seen.
Weightless and never self-assured, she counts crow caws.
Silence opens in spaces. Language at times a burden.
Smoky words drift. Her singing she says is awakening
to leaves. Eyes calm in the safety of heat coming down,
she uses pastels and paints people and movement.
Stillness, and the breath she remembers, teach her to see.
Waiting is the name of earth and dancing the name of sky.
She's drawn snakes curled and stretched, faces
betrayed. Shock and bite, the karmic twirl of her fate.
Tornado tossed, she is unknowing the drama of abuse,
the sadness of sands. Harshness traded for soft musical lines.
All is well in the cooling late afternoon of her life.
She is a gardener growing seeds. She plants sunlight,
mornings, a new patience flowering.

Manic with Depression

A manic man plants signs up and down traffic-filled streets

advocating world peace. Written on wedding wrapping paper,

blowing down sidewalks like silver birds, the words disappear.

Only sticks remain.

Depressed months later, he says, "I am the frown of my father."
One dying squirrel drops from a tree, black eye blinking.

Refusing to breathe Yin-Yang, the man cannot forget his fear.
Pigeons circle gray day; what's frozen inside cracked anew.

Needs rush through him. The golden day falls, leaves skip along asphalt.

"Someone has tampered with my car radio again."

"My roommate moved my razor."

"He moved the body wash, just dropped it on the bathtub floor!"

"Someone is out to get me from my past. Bad karma, bad, bad."

Rage swells in his eyes when I disbelieve.

His self hangs on like the last green of autumn.

His dreams misaligned then symmetrical. One intent: to live. The gray day

trips over itself. Counting pennies and thin with need, he's fixated on karma.

He has hidden his gay nature from himself for fifty years.

Misery and a bad back needing touch, have left him aware of his needs,

but Christianity has him ashamed. He lives in the tick tock of loss.

Praying, he dreams of a forever burning sun, an infinite kingdom of saints.

Eccentric

At the top of the six-foot erected plumbing pipe,
a hang glider's sail. Higher still, a bag of belongings.

The pipe welded to and perched on a bicycle pieced
together from scavenged parts.

He is proud. Vladimir shaves only half his head,
He's headed for the airport runway, blue sail
on the bike's pole flapping.

Thin and barefoot, his feet black from asphalt,
unconcerned with a stream of laughter that follows,
he says, "it's a good thing to make people laugh."

He can see beyond sky dissolving into glint.
Homeless now, once bloody with Russian army
mandatory service, he held a gun under his arm.

His wife left him for another man in America.
Work eludes him. Evicted for tearing tile up,
painting the walls with a yellow sun, he is studying

the breeze and the grief of trees. He once caught
aspen on fire barbequing a whole chicken.
Today, his bike leans against hard hip as he staggers.
He is blazing with a blue sail into the sun.

A Homeless Poet Friend Rages at the World's Lesser People

What is night but a referral to his madness?
Stone angels and gargoyles teach him
art haunts. There are visible signs, his head
full of smoggy thoughts. My silence a reception.

His trauma hides in his fury. Snow dust rises, wind
skiffs off a blanketed roof.
Light rescues bare branched trees.

His thoughts always afire, raging at delusional liberals.
Eyes crazed with disgust, he's found a world to blame.

There is a wedding of language and hate in his breath.

Words puff in the conversation of self.
Pretending he's together, thoughts muddled,
his eyes still sing a world blue.

He hasn't written a poem for years and hates
Mexicans though his name is Aparicio.

Smarter than us, after gossip he returns to grammar.
Editing sky and blackbirds, his grouchy
arguments have driven everyone away.

The Party

She is not anxious for her reputation,
        carries herself queen-like.
                Meth head and marijuana led,

raging heavy metal melodies ruin her heart.
        Camille carries herself tall,
                unashamed. Hips sway, arms swing.
        Butt large, she joggles,

snaps at her lover, orders him about,
        "Don't mess with me." Dark silver
trembles in the leaves. Shovel in hand,
        outside, she flings it at him, misses.

Clouds dim and winter
        dies on the mountainside.
Voice hoarse from screaming for days,
        face red as a super moon,
eyes alert and maddened,
        she cannot give up the past.

Weeks earlier an ambulance arrived, O.D.
        Earlier still, double pneumonia.

        Hunger and need split her. She parties,
eyes swollen, toothless mouth spitting.

Mother of seven, jailed repeatedly
        for beating other women,

today she's pounding Eloy with a shovel.

This is the way love
        works through them.

He is missing one leg, amputated
        after a drunken accident.

        He begs her to stop,
says he loves her. Banshee of rap music
        and rock, she screams an inhuman scream,

and the entire neighborhood stops.

Adopting Stepfather

Fist swatting me, startling me.

My mouth once blood with a fork inside.

Placing peas on my fork with small fingers.

Unpardonable.

My judgment of him far from dead.
Bare trees in January remind me of his death.

He too, wounded early, wounding later,
an endless chatter of pain.

His mind never stuck in repentance once?

My heart fell through his loud-mouthed
hate. And what is resolution
but a grown child accepting such noise?

Let loose breath's cadence.

Slowly beginning to move on, I am kissed
by a wet sloppy sky.

The desert no longer my debut and closure.

Heat exhaustion gone. Rain descends
cold awakening. Branches on trees hurl

winds without breaking, and I am
unrestrained in all that thunder.

Alone

My language is colloquial riff.

Elongated or staccato, our breaths
brief seasons. Birds dart to pines.

We all fold into ourselves
purple morning glories
midway through the day.

Sheltering ourselves, fully present
with suffering, we are as hesitant
words.

The early gang-rape
enough to unravel all my love?

Today's boyfriend says, "I'll leave
you alone, since you want to be
alone." Oblong scalp,

shaved blond hair, his need
for affection suffocates.

My need for distance
born early, my split mind

lifted over my broken body
an arc of sunlight.

Solitude a slow passing.
Larger than the self, I bloom light
in snow. Call it an early
frost, pansies survive it too.

What is shadow but the loss of light?
Time sometimes glimmers,
and some of us are fractured until wise.

Voice

T-shirt, eleven years old, I wear my hair up.
Shame stings me sharply; my head a foggy night.

What is real; what is not? Gazing at constellations,

praying as a child can, I hear a throbbing universe
weep. I cannot see my adoptive father's true face.

Stubbled cheeks, thin tie, and cheap boots, he looms.

Cold apparition. Hell itself burns in a child.
Throat without water,

sex unfamiliar. In my mind, my hand
against a window waving goodbye.

Train cars rumble in my head, escape a reprieve.
Fingers slam into piano keys, rush full length across.

Pent-up resentment for the past blurs. The hurried
music frantic. Pecan groves and cotton fields

remembered. Today, what's found in my voice,
music.

There is a longing in the grackles' cries.
Early Autumn's sunflowers miss bees.

What ends in violence can be a beginning.
Words learn to lighten the way sunlight takes

a picnic table on a courtyard, fall leaves scattering along the half-shaded sidewalk below.

Today my airy landscapes thrive.

There's an altitude in such falling.

Figures

Photographs of large flowers swallow the room.

She wants to be light streaming along an easel.

Every form a shadow that needs light.

She no longer sketches memories broken on abuse—

her father's backhand slamming her jaw.

Ribbons fly about her painted purple dancers now.

Two hold large gold hearts. They are nude figures

touching a backdrop of green. The canvass large.

A young man listening to her silence,

meditates on the strokes of her hand.

He disbelieves in gods and karma.

She is building herself a belief in herself.

She is speaking now. Her voice water calm.

His voice often fiery night, and he is learning

to quiet himself, hear her essence: snow on Rockies,

window unlocked in spring, doors opening.

Anxiety and Diagnosis

What does it mean to lose *myself*,
fall into the voluminous cloud of *us*?

A god damned falling—Benzodiazepine:
savior, barbiturate slowing.

It began with worry about disapproving glances,
ended with paranoia,
a distaste for slamming doors.

The word "bitch"—a reminder of childhood rape.

It's about lists and exclusions and bored loneliness.

Check and double-check assumptions we say.

I was hurried needs, Klonopin and a lack of cash.

Some of us were managing our lives
holding composed. Forget *them* I said.

Forgive myself. Forgive. Forgive.
A mental picture of a bad scene:

Police and ambulance arrived, humiliation. I was strolled out
on a gurney. I was detached from the sky.

I was the hard silver, the flat surface, mirroring myself,
then a warm blanket of seclusion.

I had only grogginess towards a nurse's
disregard. The next day a psychiatrist
began to teach me to breathe.

The Artist Addressing Violence

Some say she is derived from a single word barked into the empty black. Radio shows click through her. Feasting or fasting, she moves to the beat of old drums. She tells me she can't paint trees, only what is human: loss and praise, the illuminated journey of children. She paints figures without faces. Hands, and the perception of hands, gray in the background. She asks the universe for what's tangible: earrings, a serape, a pink beach cruiser with a wicker basket. She wants to ride, nowhere and everywhere, says she has found the rhythm of trees in a breeze. She sketches a crowd of people without eyes, builds her own canvass, wraps a towel around four stapled two by fours, says she likes the added texture. The artist saves frames found in rummage sales. As a child, she ate food out of garbage cans in Tijuana. What's shown in her hands is told in a pattern of birds circling in unison. Long assured strokes, the brush lit. She paints wildly thick rivers, bodies of women with water-like faces. She is about saving herself, keeping bad spirits at bay. Catholic and full of meaning, she is crackling goodness. She is stern about not having anything to do with therapy, refuses to drink alcohol and it's as though she's lived saying, "echo of death," "porous changes," "windblown transformations." She writes in paint, she is safe, and happy long after hospital emergency trips, blood pooling beneath her eyes as a child long after being told she was a bitch, while being raped at twelve. Years later, after she had gambled all her cash away, God came to her light, unspeakable breeze. She is certain of salvation, her soul once floating above her body, saved. Whenever I say "bitch" she asks why I can't find a better word. "Surely, you're a writer, surely you can find a better word." Any curse word an abandonment, a loss. Yet, she believes in a fight, resolve cold in her eyes.

The Singer

Some days she carries her life like a stone.
She is the jangle of art against a backdrop
of cigarette smoke. Her temper shoots at clerks,
children and strangers. Triggered by rude people,
she has no tolerance for cruelty. A maid for large
houses, words snap from lips. Vacuuming curved
patterns beneath overhead lights, a heaviness flows
down her shoulders most days. Eyes so long dim
lighten briefly with the pink dawn. With bloodshot eyes,
she's on the fringe of doubt. She must enter the center
of her own fire. The city gleams as her hips
curve to her own gusty music. Ruminating on lost
fame and beauty, a ravenous burning cuts her.
Roses sit stem-hacked in light, flaming on a glass
table. She smoothly streams notes to nowhere.
She dreams discovery— burns.
Loose hair hangs about her face. Her true persona
a B-52 rumbling through sky.

She Wishes She Never Had

She wishes she never had
oxblood red days,
loss, rivers which flowed through her
body in rough rapids.
She wants smooth currents seeking
some source that dwelled within.
She wishes she never had
refused love like a wounded
child, slapped, stunned into a sudden
submission to others. Language
a cloud, gaseous,
then pouring rain, a calm lake.
She never could find her true
name written on the wall her ancestors
built. Smoky, her eyes see fires, stars
throb, and she wanted to go one place,
but ended up here, where lizards
flick tongues and scurry under rocks
in the heat. She wishes she never walked
rolling bare blue hills, tumbleweed,
dirt roads where vultures span
wings overhead, looping towards death.
And here she is counting sparrows,
mourning doves flittering in a bare bush,
planting a fig tree in the desert of her want.

IQ Over 160?

A scalp condition wraps red about his head
like a belt. Bald and homeless, he feels
death is where it's at. Dirty, old-mannish,
admiring school girls, comments swashing
noisily, he moves down the street pot-bellied,
whistling loudly at their bodies.

She says "I" is a battle with shame.
Her house is string quartet and adagio.
She says, there are multiple truths colliding,
universes of loss. He disbelieves truth, says
shame brings the world together. Her face
symmetrical. Blonde hair flails. She bounds

across grass. Young and certain, she insists
privilege does not exist. Says a rich boy has
schizophrenia, cancerous cells rot a child.
Suffering, she asserts, is humankind's path.

But he is still poor. He blames minorities, God,
Democrats. Says if beauty is in the beholder's eye,
we are blind. He speaks past traumas in worry,
his language drowning. Lecturing that asteroid
destruction of the planet is likely, face bloated,
flushed, he is certain he is a mind-master.

MENSA member arrogant, he rambles about
his IQ. She is uninterested. He imagines them kissing,
certain about everything. He's outlandish in too youthful
combat boots and she's dainty in expensive sandals.

The mud will claim their bodies, claim their right
to deny gravity. They too will succumb to this earth.

The Prayer

She is loss's language, flat as treeless plains.
He is a drove of blackbirds, falling over asphalt.

As he beats her he screams, "Nobody said life was fair."
Telephone wires hang outside. Long hair graying, teenage

gang-rape forgiven, she is silent. Breathe
before you attempt to sing, the world tells her.

Naked force does not always win against the heart.
Afraid of his myths, her language is the magic of faith

and sunrises kissed. He only knows her nose is sharp.
His father's sermons led him to an absolute truth—

He is worthless, pitiful. What he clings to billows down,
enflamed and falling like Icarus. He later offers her aspirin.

She drifts downward, remembers him screaming,
"No talk of God—damn it." At once she sees

buds on the pecan tree outside have emerged,
understands they will grow hard, fall to ground, protect
what's soft inside. Some will break, rot black within.

*You were born a child of light's wonderful secret—
you return to the beauty you have always been.*

—Aberjhani

Night

Tonight, Mozart plays
strong and meticulous.

Love comes to us hard
when we are not taught
the language of giving.

There's a pyramid
of cigarettes in my pocket.

The gnarly tree, yellowed,
leans towards winter yawning.

Orion stretched above the house
with wild certainty.

Try and try, music comes to us
a lifting. We sketch shadows
to show light. Rivers
run through us veined, ghostly.

A wild coyote hustles
neighborhood streets scrawny.

There's nightfall in each of us.

Rubbernecking

The art of the century is to hear
sun through mulberry,
small ball of white light centered
in torn leaves. We are not
biblical? We are freedom
finding itself, here grounded
in verse as children while
the poor present alms to the poor.

We have no answers.
Some of us missed the broadcast
to success. The neighborhood
fills with unseen deep-throated
robins. Remember
what it means to be alone
we say, disliking or loving
mad streets, where the broken
fearlessly ride buses.
We cannot fix the contest
outside, even if we
rubberneck our way
through accident and luck.

Listening to Sky

There are song shells at our pink ears.

      We take apart. We break. We forsake.

Unthinkable: Girl dismembered by seventeen-year-old boy—

sky weaving a red-lit thread. We are but guests among

            dragging gray clouds.

         Tapping to the beat of stars and making music

we refuse to forget ourselves in the first snow. Newspaper stories tell us

we matter, tell us we don't matter. The dying

          churches feed us the paradox of living, the peacock's

beauty-tinged

    pride, the magnificence of errors.

        Praise more than blackberries.

        Praise more than sunshine.

At home in our graves,   we are less than politics and language.

Trust an opening of windows.

        Let go of smug selfish days.

I hear leaves scraping across pavement, falling from above at an angle.

Pumpkins half-eaten by squirrels.

                      There are secrets we keep from ourselves.

We're trying too hard;   language drifts fogged and moony.

We find our single voice in a flurry of birds.

Forgetting the self, we can finally hear the sky sigh.

Risk

For beauty is nothing but the beginning of terror,
which we are still just able to endure,
and we are so awed because it serenely disdains to annihilate us.
Every angel is terrifying. —Rilke

The mystic whispered, "It's time you

took a risk. You are a mountain, immovable

amidst storms." *I* is the space

within the light of now. The teacher said,

"You have no idea how much power you have."

Angels are not terrifying, balanced

on the snow-covered steeps of my dreams.

I am sunset in the west. Sacred

scrolls were lost in the desert hills of a bad

childhood. Rivers drowned my manuscripts

of loss, but I am ready to accept

shadow and sun. Wings of imaginary angels

wrap me in the sky, which moves unpredictably

always. Lightning scrawls across as if

breaking the world. I imagine crows falling.

I am letting go shame, risking my story. Dreamers

cross borders, tigers careen against bloody antelope,

and today is my prayer, my move. Since I was a child,

everyone has said to forget the body.

I am as air, atoms full of emptiness, expansion.

Solidity a mirage. Nothing is harder than saying

goodbye to myself.

The Laugh

The wind-worry of my life rustles. I bend like a wounded
sapling, dream of bonsai trees and laughter, I will learn
not to pout. Christians gather hungry, forcing away doubt.

Stars erupt in our bodies. Wet-necked geese lumber.
Maple leaves swat the sky, and we shape our own lives.
We know the sky, lit at times, unknowingly gives us light.

Understand, it may be in the slowness, the way a star
bursts within you. It may be obsessive, the way the sun
calls your name. You too lost and seeking the rowboat
of forgiveness. We are called to direct our own
wondrous collisions. Fate or flurry,

our nurturing mothers admit us into this theatre-dream,
and we are all artists
seeking image and sound. We are one essence
learning to forget ourselves.

We Believe in Kindness Because It's Hard to Die

And here we are breathing for a time. Ice comes soon enough:
struck cars, bruised tailbones, sirens in dark. Each moment
a police officer at the door. The gun black, heavy in the holster,
a baton moving in sync with a leg. Each moment a hibiscus
opening briefly to life.

We don't remember currents that run through us wildly
and forget to study our own breath.

Yin and Yang circle us daily.
Pain and suffering are conferred on us,

and we are not masters of our world. We half understand
the divine within us, sunlight streaming on our skin.
We are beauty evolved, creation done. Our task
is finishing well. Leaves rush along sidewalks
and grass, spot their way to mulch.

In the end, we cannot swallow. Our feet turn purplish gray, throats
burn, swallowing impossible. Age and death twist about us,
garter snakes mating before a storm. The end slithers, presses up
our bodies, a cold-blooded lover.

Casualties

The loud ruckus in our foreheads
keeps us talking. Yet the brimming trees
speak for us all. An angelic boy, star of David
tattooed on his chest, blood on his gun,

thinks an idea will help release the world.
Another boy with a prayer towards the East
straps a bomb to his guts.

Explosive galaxies roam the bodies of the hated
poor. Light is the living universe reflected within.

Perception makes us gods of light.
We are essentially empty
as the dark between stars, yet full Super Nova.

We walk through the twilight of ourselves.

Our story is the story of both boys:
blood and light, ancient and new.

We are all full of questions and lies.
And who or what is listening to our dialogue?

We want to believe the light
but fear we are nothing
but soil and night.

The Witness

Our mistakes crack open. Each leaf
veined distinctly,

and we are star-made music makers,
fingerprinted originality.

This is expansion: to stand as One with all.

The mountains a dense
explosion of trees.

Night comes to us sexy,
whispers to us about belief in light.

Words tumble from us. Honesty, a naked
falling.

We linger in the source of gardens.

For two hundred thousand years,
we have been deaf.

We forget meaning, our storylines
repeat the rhythm of our breaking.

The soul is without weight in the end.

We must find the calm witness
within that observes the self

quietly, the child laughing
in a flurry of light.

The Hummingbird

There will be exploding
stars during the Armageddon
of my soul. I will gather all my petty
glooms, burn them for an urn. The flash
will fizzle like a sparkler. I will seek
my final pulse and brief light.
I will die with dilating eyes,
listening to an imaginary wind, watch
streams glimmer with small stars. Lovers
will moan inside my heart. I will swim
frothy waters. Trees will loom perfectly irregular,
saplings will survive their traumas.
If longevity will have me, my hands
will tremble with thick blue veins.
Addendums to my past will not be added.
Poets will not write poems for me, painters
will pass by. I will no longer doubt the God
of childhood. They will place a bible in my
clasped hands. I will remember the red
hummingbird I saw today hovering on the path
before my heart, uninterested in my
procession towards silence.

Clouds and Sapling

after W. S. Merwin

Men think they are superior to grass.

Touch and conversation run the edges of our

separateness. Community smaller than we

imagine. Nothing hurts the Eastern horizon today.

To the west, blue mountains snow covered in June.

Rebirth, some say, begins with bloodletting.

The past is often bruised.

Beams of one distant star startle us. No

surprise we travel hard corners.

Finding the trauma, turning its sharp key,

opens the way for splendor. We break open, briefly

lit clouds over a darkening storm.

We fall, white ash over asphalt streets in winter,

begin again, sapling and dandelion

bursting through what seems an unbreakable black.

Prayer for this Clay Earth

Teach us the language of spilling out of ourselves.

Teach us the language of moon, rain beating on cheeks, divinity lighting our eyes.   Teach us nothing

conceptual about fear, only how it concretely tightens chests, trembles down arms.   Teach us fiery music,

the silence of trees, currents of sky and water.

Teach us to rebuke the language of drowning,
to hold close breath and pulse of the body—

Teach us healing above all, soothing the center
of our being. Teach us dark

solitude without longing.

Mud

I am speaking the language of curanderas,
old hymns. My family's prayers
crowd the church.

A throng of stars with a red
supermoon hangs above.
A dying man says

we are all divine. We are Gods of earth,
mud and worm, watching blue birds
cackle, robins snap black

worms from the damp earth.
Hunger compels us to kill something.
We listen to lyrics,

hoping to become civilized and smooth.
The *I* sits at the periphery of loss.

Stars at the edge of night
form a roof over the Southwest.

Some days we are impatient
with the mud of ourselves.

Murky, we are listing our own corruptions,
seeking the eyes of others for redemption.

We are electric charging presences.
Some say our energy moves on,
manifests as something else.

Energy never disappears. We are as branch, fire and wind. All the while there's a tornado stirring in our single heart.

Finding Water

Deserts irrigated with labor, we do not
understand our own

messages. Cup-bearers,
givers of water, we can

drown in the past,
drunks holding signs,

begging for liquor money,
forsaking our own names.

We are fiery assurances, aquifers,
mountain streams. What shapes us

runs inexhaustible,
necessary. There is no meaningless

voice in suffering. No one will
remember the day we die in the end.

In solitude heat breaks over our backs,
yet all of us loving the musical sound of birds.

The Transgression

We all unfold as music.

Our desire appears each morning.

It is white-lit, bare-branched hunger for the entire sky.

Dogs bark at a man with a leaf blower.

Doors open, close. My mind, and yours, lit by sun.

Ravens caw, an unkindness tumults in the blue.

We feel we learn our traumas too late, but we are as

children. Our heart, some days, an orchestra suddenly

aflame. Closing our eyes, we see our salmon-lit dawn,

and it is no transgression to look towards

ourselves with awe..

Sheryl Luna's first collection, *Pity the Drowned Horses*, won the inaugural Andrés Montoya Poetry Prize for emerging Latino/a poets (University of Notre Dame Press, 2005). Her second book of poetry, *Seven*, was a runner up for the Ernest Sandeen Poetry Prize. She has been awarded fellowships from Yaddo, Anderson Center, Ragdale Foundation, and Canto Mundo. She received the Alfredo Cisneros del Moral Foundation Award from Sandra Cisneros in 2008. Her poems have appeared in *Poetry*, *Georgia Review*, *Prairie Schooner*, *Poetry Northwest*, *Puerto del Sol*, *Kalliope*, and *Notre Dame Review*, among others.

www.ingramcontent.com/pod-product-compliance
Lightning Source LLC
Chambersburg PA
CBHW050917160426
43194CB00011B/2447